This book is a

Gift

From

....

To

....

Date

....

May God bless you through this book

Prayers to overcome an evil habit

PRAYERS TO OVERCOME AN EVIL HABIT

PRAYERS TO OVERCOME AN EVIL HABIT

Copyright © 2014

PRAYER M. MADUEKE

ISBN:

Prayer Publications

Unless otherwise indicated, all Scripture quotations are taken from the King James Version of the Bible, and used by permission. All emphasis within quotations is the author's additions.

First Edition, 2014

For further information of permission

1 Babatunde close, off Olaitan Street, Surulere, Lagos, Nigeria
+234 803 353 0599
Email: pastor@prayermadueke.com,
Website: www.prayermadueke.com

Dedication

This book is dedicated to people who are trusting God to overcome all forms of evil character and habits. The Lord who sees your sincere dedication will answer your prayers Amen.

Prayers to overcome an evil habit

BOOK OVERVIEW

PRAYERS TO OVERCOME AN EVIL HABIT

- *Discerning evil characters*
- *The old man*
- *Putting on new apparel*

DISCERNING EVIL CHARACTERS

Character is like apparel, which every man or woman wears that cannot be hidden for too long. This is true because character is a set of qualities that make somebody or something distinctive, especially somebody's qualities of mind and feeling. No matter how well a mad person dresses, once he exhibits his or her character, you would discern at once that the fellow has mental problem.

Likewise, character distinguishes a new man from an old man. In professional careers, dresses are used to distinguish professions. A footballer, police officer, nurse, soldier and security guard would wear a uniform that suits their profession.

> *"But now ye also put off all these; anger, wrath, malice, blasphemy, filthy communication out of your mouth. Lie not one to another, seeing that ye have put off the old man with his deeds; And have put on the new man, which is renewed in knowledge after the image of him that created him: Where there is neither Greek nor Jew, circumcision nor uncircumcision, Barbarian, Scythian, bond nor free: but Christ is all, and in all"* (Colossians 3:8-11).

There are certain characters that when you fail to put off, no matter how glorious your destiny is, they would still ruin your life. Your character identifies you with some group of people in the world. The world is a uniformed society and once you display your character, it aligns you with a certain group of people. As you can rightly tell what people do by observing the kind of clothes they wear on daily basis, you can also classify a certain group of people by their habits.

2

I define an evil group as a group of people that put on similar evil characters and placed themselves under an evil leadership (*See* 2 Corinthians 4:4).

Many people in the world have consciously placed themselves under the leadership of the god of this world. For such people, their minds have been blinded not to believe the gospel of Christ that can transform their lives and characters. As a result, they remain under the control of the devil.

Be mindful also that styles of clothes believers wear and stickers they put on their cars and houses they build are not enough to distinguish true Christians. What distinguishes true Christians is the spirit that dwells in them. By the fruits of their characters, you will know them. Anyone who is not born-again is bound to be at the mercy of evil habits or characters. It is probable that such persons' understanding remains darkened, and their hearts deceitful and desperately wicked.

> *"Having the understanding darkened, being alienated from the life of God through the ignorance that is in them, because of the blindness of their heart"* (Ephesians 4:18).

> *"Thus said the LORD unto me; Go and stand in the gate of the children of the people, whereby the kings of Judah come in, and by the which they go out, and in all the gates of Jerusalem"* (Jeremiah 17:19).

> *"Unto the pure all things* are *pure: but unto them that are defiled and unbelieving is nothing pure; but even their mind and conscience is defiled"* (Titus 1:15).

3

"Is any man called being circumcised? Let him not become uncircumcised. Is any called in uncircumcision? Let him not be circumcised" (1 Corinthians 7:18).

The heart and mind of an unbeliever are homes to all manner of bad characters and are desperate to do evil because his conscience is deceitful and defiled. His mind remains a boiling pot of all manner of evil that are desperately waiting for an opportunity to be displayed. The will of such a person remains enslaved because the root of sin, which is the old man, is very active. The body of sin is deeply rooted in his foundation. The body of can only be destroyed when we crucify our old man on the cross of Jesus.

"Knowing this, that our old man is crucified with him, that the body of sin might be destroyed, that henceforth we should not serve sin" (Romans 6:6).

"That ye put off concerning the former conversation the old man, which is corrupt according to the deceitful lusts" (Ephesians 4:22).

"Lie not one to another, seeing that ye have put off the old man with his deeds" (Colossians 3:9).

All his actions are carnal because he has carnal mind, the mind of flesh that is filled with all manner of filthiness and dominated by evil habits.

"[7]Because the carnal mind is enmity against God: for it is not subject to the law of God, neither indeed can be. [8]So then they that are in the flesh cannot please God. [9]But ye are not in the flesh, but in the Spirit, if so is that the Spirit of God dwells in you. Now if any man has not the Spirit

of Christ, he is none of his. [12]Therefore, brethren, we are debtors, not to the flesh, to live after the flesh. [13]For if ye live after the flesh, ye shall die: but if ye through the Spirit do mortify the deeds of the body, ye shall live" (Romans 8:7-9, 12-13).

Evil habit is a dominating tyrant. A hereditary evil is an inward enemy that you need to deal with urgently. Evil habit corrupts your moral nature and is able to waste a greatly destined person and send such person to hell fire. You cannot afford to take evil characters lightly.

"If so be that ye have heard him, and have been taught by him, as the truth is in Jesus: That ye put off concerning the former conversation the old man, which is corrupt according to the deceitful lusts; And be renewed in the spirit of your mind; And that ye put on the new man, which after God is created in righteousness and true holiness. Wherefore putting away lying, speaks every man truth with his neighbor: for we are members one of another. Be ye angry, and sin not: let not the sun goes down upon your wrath: Neither give place to the devil. Let him that stole steal no more: but rather let him labor, working with his hands the thing, which is good, that he may have to give to him that needed. Let no corrupt communication proceed out of your mouth, but that, which is good to the use of edifying, that it may minister grace unto the hearers. And grieve not the holy Spirit of God, whereby ye are sealed unto the day of redemption. Let all bitterness, and wrath, and anger, and clamor, and evil speaking, be put away from you, with all malice: And be ye kind one to another, tenderhearted, forgiving one

5

another, even as God for Christ's sake hath forgiven you" (<u>Ephesians 4:21-32</u>).

THE OLD MAN

A good number of Christians attend churches regularly and assume the title "Christian" without really knowing the weight and authority a Christian possesses. A Christian is one who had an encounter with Christ and has become a new creature by His grace. Old things have passed away, and a new relationship with God and his fellow man established.

The old man is the natural self that has the resemblance of Adam. It is still under the curse of Adam's sin. The difference between the old and new man is that while the old man remains under the law of sin and death, the new man remains under the law of the Spirit and life.

> *"Therefore if any man be in Christ, he is a new creature: old things are passed away; behold, all things are become new"* (2 Corinthians 5:17).

> *"And when he had found him, he brought him unto Antioch. In addition, it happened, that a whole year they assembled themselves with the church, and taught much people. And the disciples were called Christians first in Antioch"* (Acts 11:26).

Many people fill their lives with religious activities when the deeds of the old man constantly overrun their lives. Such people do not have any place for God in the lives.

7

CHARACTERISTICS OF THE OLD MAN

LIES: To lie is to say something that is not true in a conscious effort to deceive somebody. The bible called devil the father of all lies. Unfortunately, lying has become a way of life for so many Christians. Lying is an evil habit that you must put off at once if you want to put on the garment of righteousness. Make it a duty to speak the truth at all times no matter the consequence.

> *"Wherefore putting away lying, speaks every man truth with his neighbor: for we are members one of another"* (<u>Ephesians 4:25</u>).

> *"For the rich men thereof are full of violence, and the inhabitants thereof have spoken lies, and their tongue is deceitful in their mouth"* (<u>Micah 6:12</u>).

> *"Their throat is an open sepulcher; with their tongues they have used deceit; the poison of asps is under their lips"* (<u>Romans 3:13</u>).

Truth is the character of true Christians all over the world. God hates lies and deceit because they are not His nature, but the nature of the devil. You cannot claim to be a Christian and tell lies to deceive your neighbor. A tongue that tells lies is defiled and needs urgent New Testament deliverance. Some Christians give untrue testimonies to deceive themselves. Such lies are the character of the devil. You cannot tell lies to please God. It is not possible.

> *"Now the Spirit speaketh expressly, that in the latter times some shall depart from the faith, giving heed to seducing spirits, and doctrines of devils; Speaking lies in hypocrisy; having their conscience seared with a hot iron"* (<u>1 Timothy 4:1-2</u>).

"But the fearful, and unbelieving, and the abominable, and murderers, and whoremongers, and sorcerers, and idolaters, and all liars, shall have their part in the lake which burneth with fire and brimstone: which is the second death" (Revelation 21:8).

God will judge all lies no matter who is involved. Preachers must courageously rebuke and preach against lies. It is heartbreaking for a preacher or a leader to encourage lies. God would judge these are categories of people fiercely –

- **Unbelievers** (*See* John 3:18-20, 36).

- **Defilers** (*See* Leviticus 18:21-27; Deuteronomy 22:5; Proverbs 6:16-19).

- **Murderers** (*See* 1 John 3:15).

- **Whoremongers, fornicators, adulterers** (*See* Matthew 5:27-30).

- **Sorcerers, witches and people using familiar spirits** (*See* Deuteronomy 18:914; 1 Samuel 28:5-11; 1 Chronicles 10:13-14; Isaiah 8:19).

- **Idolaters** (*See* Exodus 20:3-5; 1 John 5:21).

- **Liars** (*See* Revelation 21:27, 8; 22:15).

God will banish sinners from his presence forever and from the holy city. He will forever cast them into the lake of fire. They cannot stain or desecrate heaven.

STEALING: Grabbing something that belongs to another person illegally is not the character of a child of God. The grace to work and provide for oneself has been given to all men. If you have been providing for your family through stealing, it is time for you to stop. Look for a job and work with your hands in a right way. Many lazy people complain a lot for lack of jobs, but if you are diligent and determined, you will discover your talent soon in the name of Jesus.

"Let him that stole steal no more: but rather let him labor, working with his hands the thing, which is good, that he may have to give to him that needed" (Ephesians 4:28).

"Ye shall not steal, neither deal falsely, neither lie one to another. [13]Thou shall not defraud thy neighbor, neither rob him: the wages of him that is hired shall not abide with thee all night until the morning" (Leviticus 19:11, 13).

"For I the LORD love judgment, I hate robbery for burnt offering; and I will direct their work in truth, and I will make an everlasting covenant with them" (Isaiah 61:8).

"Will ye steal, murder, and commit adultery, and swear falsely, and burn incense unto Baal, and walk after other gods whom ye know not" (Jeremiah 7:9).

God gave all men diverse talents. Every serious minded person would discover his or her talent and use it to the glory of God. The reason why people steal and defraud others is that they have failed to discover their rightful places in life. No one can be happy without discovering his place in life. If you do not get to a God's ordained place for your life, you can never fulfill your destiny, no matter how much wealth you gather.

If you feel dissatisfied in the place you are right now, you could have stolen another person's place. When you fail to position yourself rightly, you may occupy another person's position. If you are paying people that work for you less that they deserve, you are stealing from them. If you receive reward for what you did not labor for, you are also stealing. When you did no work but receive wages, you are stealing. You need to start doing something. If what you are doing does not give you joy, you may be in a wrong position. If you pray with sincere heart and determination, God will give you a suitable job. Everyone on earth has a position. God cannot create you if he has no place for you to occupy on earth.

"Verily, verily, I say unto you, He that entereth not by the door into the sheepfold, but climbeth up some other way, the same is a thief and a robber" (John 10:1).

"And it came to pass after this, that Absalom prepared him chariots and horses, and fifty men to run before him. And Absalom rose up early, and stood beside the way of the gate: and it was so, that when any man that had a controversy came to the king for judgment, then Absalom called unto him, and said, Of what city art thou? In addition, he said, Thy servant is of one of the tribes of Israel. And Absalom said unto him, See, thy matters are good and right; but there is no man deputed of the king to hear thee. Absalom said moreover, Oh that I were made judge in the land, that every man which hath any suit or cause might come unto me, and I would do him justice! And it was so, that when any man came nigh to him to do him obeisance, he put forth his hand, and took him, and kissed him. And on this manner did Absalom to all Israel that came to the king for judgment: so Absalom stole the hearts of the men of Israel" (2 Samuel 15:1-6).

When you live your life by robbing others, you will definitely not have rest or good success. Before God created the world, He has positioned everything on earth the way they are supposed to be. You cannot come to this earth and begin to misplace things. God has placed people in their rightful places. Therefore, no one can succeed through robbery. It is foolishness to believe that if you do wrong, God will not judge you or ask you why. Every godly person must hate what God hates and love what God loves.

It is also foolishness and deceit to imagine that you are a child of God while you steal, murder, commit adultery, swear falsely, burn incense to Baal, walk after other gods and do all manner of evil things. If you live your life by doing these things, then you are a thief before God. Absalom died because he wanted the throne of his father at all cost. You might be destined for an earthly throne, but if you want it at all cost, you will surely fail. When you deceive other people, you are a thief and you must surely pay for whatever that you steal.

EVIL SPEAKING: To speak evil about other people is evil itself. It is destructive and you must put it off from your life once you are born-again. You cannot say that you are a child of God when you continue speaking evil of other people. It is very deadly and destructive.

> *"Let no corrupt communication proceed out of your mouth, but that which is good to the use of edifying, that it may minister grace unto the hearers"* (Ephesians 4:29).

> *"The LORD shall cut off all flattering lips, and the tongue that speaketh proud things"* (Psalms 12:3).

"Thy tongue deviseth mischiefs; like a sharp razor, working deceitfully. Thou lovest evil more than good; and *lying rather than to speak righteousness. Selah. Thou lovest all devouring words, O* thou *deceitful tongue"* (Psalms 52:2-4).

Corruption is the work of the devil. When your mouth is corrupt, it becomes easier to engage in evil speaking. A born-again Christian asks for grace to overcome speaking evil of people at all times. It is rather strange that many people become Christians, yet they refuse to behave like Christ. They claim to be born-again but operate on their old selves, which is the carnal self. This is strange.

Corrupt communication is of the devil and his children. A good word that edifies and ministers grace to the hearer comes from God. Through your communication, people can tell where you belong. Flattering lips in God's house are working for the devil. The tongues that speak proudly will be cut off. You need to watch your tongue to prove which kingdom you belong to. You can do it yourself and judge rightly.

"An ungodly man diggeth up evil: and in his lips there is *as a burning fire. A forward man soweth strife: and a whisperer separateth chief friends"* (Proverbs 16:27-28).

"The words of a talebearer are *as wounds, and they go down into the innermost parts of the belly. Burning lips and a wicked heart* are as *a potsherd covered with silver dross. He that hated dissembleth with his lips, and layeth up deceit within him; When he speaketh fair, believes him not: for* there are *seven abominations in his*

heart. Whose *hatred is covered by deceit, his wickedness shall be showed before the* whole *congregation"* (Proverbs 26:22-26).

When you use your tongue to device iniquity, you have become an evil speaker. If you do not have control over what comes out of your mouth, you are also an evil speaker. If your words are sharp like a razor and full of deceit, you are an evil speaker. If you love evil more than good, you are an evil speaker. If you are comfortable and happy when you tell lies, no matter what position you occupy in the body of Christ, you are a child of the devil. If you chose to speak lies when you know the truth, you are an agent of the devil.

What you need is deliverance that comes from Christ. You need help because God did not create you to work for the devil. A true child of God would hate lies and evil speaking. God did not create you so that you can use your tongue to devour others. However, it could not be your fault because all men are born with evil tongues. However, you would be held responsible only when you refuse to accept deliverance and salvation that Jesus gives to all men freely. Jesus wants to help you acquire a new inheritance in the spirit.

"Come unto me, all ye that labor and are heavy laden and I will give you rest. Take my yoke upon you, and learn of me; for I am meek and lowly in heart: and ye shall find rest unto your souls. For my yoke is easy, and my burden is light" (Matthew 11:28-30).

There are people God called ungodly. How do we know such people when we see them? The Lord said they dig up evil; they look for trouble and use their lips to spread such evil like a burning fire. They use their speeches to sow strife and separate close friends. Evil speaking is a very dangerous thing. If you do not put them away from your life, they will steal your peace and joy forever. God hates evil speaking and conspiracy.

> *"O generation of vipers, how can ye, being evil, speaks good things? For out of the abundance of the heart the mouth speaketh. A good man out of the good treasure of the heart bringeth forth good things: and an evil man out of the evil treasure bringeth forth evil things. But I say unto you, That every idle word that men shall speak, they shall give account thereof in the Day of Judgment. For by thy words thou shall be justified, and by thy words thou shall be condemned"* (Matthew 12:34-37).

The sin of evil speaking can kills more people than guns and wars do. Miriam and Aaron, Moses elder sister and brother, spoke evil against Moses and God judged them. Miriam became a leper. Likewise, the ten spies were not allowed to enter the land of Canaan for the second time for delivering an evil judgment.

Korah, Dothan and Abiriam perished with all their family members for speaking evil. The ground opened and swallowed them alive. God hates evil speaking. The words of an evil speaker or talebearer are like wounds that go down into the innermost parts of the stomach. An injury inside the stomach is one of the most painful and disturbing wounds one can bear. The truth is that when you reject Christ, you cannot avoid evil speaking. Evil speaking is full of idle words. Keep in mind that you must give account of every evil intent, purpose and deed and idle word, which you did not repent of.

BITTERNESS AND WRATH: Bitterness and wrath are evidences that someone lacks the character of God. When the love of God resonates in your life, no amount of indignities, gossips and opposition can cause you to hate or become bitter. You will not allow bitterness or wrath to put you off the love of Christ.

"Let all bitterness, and wrath, and anger, and clamor, and evil speaking, be put away from you, with all malice" (Ephesians 4:31).

"Looking diligently lest any man fail of the grace of God; lest any root of bitterness springing up trouble you, and there by many be defiled; Lest there be any fornicator, or profane person, as Esau, who for one morsel of meat sold his birthright. For ye know how that afterward, when he would have inherited the blessing, he was rejected: for he found no place of repentance, though he sought it carefully with tears" (Hebrews 12:15-17).

Believers who have dealt with bitterness in their lives ought to do everything possible not to entangle themselves in bitterness again. This is because when you fall into bitterness and wrath the second time, the bondage might become double.

"But if ye have bitter envying and strife in your hearts, glory not, and lie not against the truth. This wisdom descendeth not from above, but is earthly, sensual, and devilish. For where envying and strife is, there is confusion and every evil work" (James 3:14-16).

God hates bitterness and no one who wishes to please God would entertain bitterness and wrath. Children of God are known for being peaceful, gentle and generous, full of mercy and bearing good fruits. Children of God are impartial and are not hypocrites.

ANGER AND CLAMOR: Anger destroys all form of kindness and peace. Anger denied Moses entry into the Promised Land. If not controlled, anger can waste a whole city. Anger incites people to react violently without considering the consequences. Anger brings hatred, retaliation and resorts to violence. However, the Scriptures implored us to:

"Let all bitterness, and wrath, and anger, and clamor, and evil speaking, be put away from you, with all malice" (Ephesians 4:31).

"Cease from anger, and forsake wrath: fret not thyself in any wise to do evil" (Psalms 37:8).

"But whoso committed adultery with a woman lacketh understanding: he that doeth it destroyed his own soul" (Proverbs 6:32).

"But I say unto you, That whosoever is angry with his brother without a cause shall be in danger of the judgment: and whosoever shall say to his brother, Racas, shall be in danger of the council: but whosoever shall say, Thou fool, shall be in danger of hell fire" (Matthew 5:22).

You must put away these things before you can convince people that you are a Christian. God commanded all His children to cease from anger and forsake wrath. Anything less than that is demonic and unacceptable by God. Anger puts people in the danger of eternal damnation.

"But now ye also put off all these; anger, wrath, malice, blasphemy, filthy communication out of your mouth" (Colossians 3:8).

17

"Wherefore laying aside all malice, and all guile, and hypocrisies, and envies, and all evil speaking" (1 Peter 2:1).

To keep malice and claim to be a child of God is contradictory. You must lay aside all forms of evil if you really want to be a friend of God. Pray fervently against these dangerous evil habits. Christians are not to grieve the Holy Spirit.

"And grieve not the Holy Spirit of God, whereby ye are sealed unto the day of redemption" (Ephesians 4:30).

"But they rebelled, and vexed his Holy Spirit: therefore he was turned to be their enemy, and he fought against them" (Isaiah 63:10).

"But Peter said, Ananias, why hath Satan filled thine heart to lie to the Holy Ghost, and to keep back part of the price of the land?" (Acts 5:3).

"Ye stiff-necked and uncircumcised in heart and ears, ye do always resist the Holy Ghost: as your fathers did, so do ye" (Acts 7:51).

When a Christian fornicates or commits adultery, he grieves the Holy Spirit (*See* Ephesians 5:3, Acts 15:28-29; Colossians 3:5).

When a Christian does anything unclean, he grieves the Holy Spirit (*See* 1 Thessalonians 4:7, Ephesians 5:3; Romans 1:23-24; 6:21).

When a Christian becomes covetous, he grieves the Holy Spirit (*See* Ephesians 5:3; Exodus 20:17; Ezekiel 33:31; Luke 12:15).

When a Christian becomes filthy and begins to live a filthy life, he grieves the Holy Spirit (*See* Ephesians 5:4; James 1:21; 2 Peter 2:10; Psalms 53:1-4).

When a Christian indulges in foolish talking, he grieves the Holy Spirit (*See* Ephesians 5:4; James 1:26-27; Proverbs 10:19; 1 Peter 3:10).

When a Christian backslides, he grieves the Holy Spirit (*See* Proverbs 26:18-19).

Many professing Christians have deviated from the standards of the Bible. However, the Word of God still stands sure. These things should not be named among Christians. Christians are not to have fellowship with darkness but are to be filled with the Holy Spirit. The Holy Spirit makes Christianity sweet and refreshing. Any character that opposes God's righteousness is an evil character that must not be found in your life.

PUTTING ON NEW APPAREL

When you become a Christian, a miracle takes place. The old man (*flesh*) dies and gives place to a new man (*spirit*). So-called Christians who retain the old man and his deeds cannot exercise authority over the old man and his activities. You have to put off the old man and all his activities before you can reign over him.

> *"But now ye also put off all these; anger, wrath, malice, blasphemy, filthy communication out of your mouth. Lie not one to another, seeing that ye have put off the old man with his deeds"* (Colossians 3:8-9).

> *"Knowing this, that our old man is crucified with him, that the body of sin might be destroyed, that henceforth we should not serve sin"* (Romans 6:6).

> *"Forasmuch then as Christ hath suffered for us in the flesh, arm yourselves likewise with the same mind: for he that hath suffered in the flesh hath ceased from sin; That he no longer should live the rest of his time in the flesh to the lusts of men, but to the will of God. For the time past of our life may suffice us to have wrought the will of the Gentiles, when we walked in lasciviousness, lusts, excess of wine, revellings, banqueting, and abominable idolatries: Wherein they think it strange that ye run not with them to the same excess of riot, speaking evil of you"* (1 Peter 4:1-4).

You must put off characters of the old man, which include anger, wrath, malice, blasphemy, filthy communication, lies, etc. When you become a new

20

creature (*born of the Spirit*), filled with the power of the spirit, you have control and authority over your old nature, where devil operates. Then you can exercise authority over the flesh and all its appearances.

If you have a father who is a drunkard, you may need to exercise your spiritual power over him sometimes. For instance, when he becomes drunk and insists that he will drive, you would discern that if he does, he might possibly have an accident and kill himself. If he disagrees with your pleas and insists on driving under the influence of alcohol, what you need to do is to get ready spiritually, put on your new apparel as a police officer and prepare for action. If he speeds more than you would permit, you raise your hand of authority and stop him.

At that point, you no longer act as his son or his daughter. You are a representative of a kingdom of God and disobedience is not acceptable in the kingdom of your Father, who is in heaven. Do you know that you are a representative of heaven and an ambassador of Christ? Do you know that you belong to a royal priesthood? As a Christian, the old man of drunkenness and evil desires can no longer push you around. You are no longer under the control of the works of the flesh. Instead, they are under your control.

> *"That ye put off concerning the former conversation the old man, which is corrupt according to the deceitful lusts; And be renewed in the spirit of your mind; And that ye put on the new man, which after God is created in righteousness and true holiness. Wherefore putting away lying, speaks every man truth with his neighbor: for we are members one of another. Be ye angry, and sin not: let not the sun goes*

21

down upon your wrath: Neither give place to the devil. Let him that stole steal no more: but rather let him labor, working with his hands the thing, which is good, that he may have to give to him that needed. Let no corrupt communication proceed out of your mouth, but that, which is good to the use of edifying, that it may minister grace unto the hearers. And grieve not the holy Spirit of God, whereby ye are sealed unto the day of redemption. Let all bitterness, and wrath, and anger, and clamor, and evil speaking, be put away from you, with all malice: And be ye kind one to another, tenderhearted, forgiving one another, even as God for Christ's sake hath forgiven you" (Ephesians 4:22-32).

"Now the works of the flesh are manifest, which are these; Adultery, fornication, uncleanness, lasciviousness, Idolatry, witchcraft, hatred, variance, emulations, wrath, strife, seditions, heresies, Envyings, murders, drunkenness, revellings, and such like: of the which I tell you before, as I have also told you in time past, that they which do such things shall not inherit the kingdom of God" (Galatians 5:19-21).

When you fail to recognize and assume your rights and authority as a new man of the spirit, you would remain at the mercy of the flesh (*old man*). You continue to wear your old apparel. As a Christian, you must put off the old garments of sin and flesh. A divine miracle took place immediately you were born-again. You ceased to belong to the old man. You became a new man of the spirit. Therefore, as a new man you must not respond to the desires of the flesh such as fornication, evil desires, anger, uncleanness, covetousness, wrath, malice, inordinate affection, filthiness, blasphemes, lying, etc.

Thank You So Much!

Beloved, I hope you enjoyed this book as much as I believe God has touched your heart today. I cannot thank you enough for your continued support for this prayer ministry.

I appreciate you so much for taking out time to read this wonderful prayer book, and if you have an extra second, I would love to hear what you think about this book.

Please, do share your testimonies with me by sending emails to pastor@prayermadueke.com, or through the social media at www.facebook.com/prayer.madueke. I invite you also to www.prayermadueke.com to view other books I have written on various issues of life, especially on marriage, family, sexual problems and money.

I will be delighted to partner with you in organized crusades, ceremonies, marriages and Marriage seminars, special events, church ministration and fellowship for the advancement of God's Kingdom here on earth.

Thank you again, and I wish you success in your life.

God bless you.

In Christ,

Prayer M. Madueke

OTHER BOOKS BY PRAYER M. MADUEKE

- *21/40 Nights Of Decrees And Your Enemies Will Surrender*
- *Confront And Conquer*
- *Tears in Prison*
- *35 Special Dangerous Decrees*
- *The Reality of Spirit Marriage*
- *Queen of Heaven*
- *Leviathan the Beast*
- *100 Days Prayer To Wake Up Your Lazarus*
- *Dangerous Decrees To Destroy Your Destroyers*
- *The spirit of Christmas*
- *More Kingdoms To Conquer*
- *Your Dream Directory*
- *The Sword Of New Testament Deliverance*
- *Alphabetic Battle For Unmerited Favors*
- *Alphabetic Character Deliverance*
- *Holiness*
- *The Witchcraft Of The Woman That Sits Upon Many Waters*
- *The Operations Of The Woman That Sits Upon Many Waters*
- *Powers To Pray Once And Receive Answers*
- *Prayer Riots To Overthrow Divorce*
- *Prayers To Get Married Happily*
- *Prayers To Keep Your Marriage Out of Troubles*
- *Prayers For Conception And Power To Retain*
- *Prayer Retreat – Prayers to Possess Your Year*
- *Prayers for Nation Building*
- *Organized student in a disorganized school*
- *Welcome to Campus*
- *Alone with God (10 series)*

CONTACTS

AFRICA
#1 Babatunde close,
Off Olaitan Street, Surulere
Lagos, Nigeria
+234 803 353 0599
pastor@prayermadueke.com

#Plot 1791, No. 3 Ijero Close,
Flat 2, Area 1,
Garki 1 - FCT, Abuja
+234 807 065 4159

IRELAND
Ps Emmanuel Oko
#84 Thornfield Square
Cloudalkin D22
Ireland
Tel: +353 872 820 909, +353 872 977 422
aghaoko2003@yahoo.com

EUROPE/SCHENGEN
Collins Kwame
#46 Felton Road
Barking
Essex IG11 7XZ GB
Tel: +44 208 507 8083, +44 787 703 2386, +44 780 703
6916
aghaoko2003@yahoo.com

Made in United States
North Haven, CT
23 December 2024